Wyoming

A Buddy Book
by
Julie Murray

ABDO
Publishing Company

VISIT US AT

www.abdopub.com

Published by ABDO Publishing Company, 4940 Viking Drive, Edina, Minnesota 55435.

Copyright © 2006 by Abdo Consulting Group, Inc. International copyrights reserved in all countries. No part of this book may be reproduced in any form without written permission from the publisher. Buddy Books™ is a trademark and logo of ABDO Publishing Company.

Printed in the United States.

Edited by: Sarah Tieck
Contributing Editor: Michael P. Goecke
Graphic Design: Deb Coldiron, Maria Hosley
Image Research: Sarah Tieck
Photographs: AP/Wide World, Clipart.com, Getty Images, One Mile Up, Photodisc

Library of Congress Cataloging-in-Publication Data

Murray, Julie, 1969-
   Wyoming / Julie Murray.
      p. cm. — (The United States)
   Includes index.
      Contents: A snapshot of Wyoming — Where is Wyoming? — All about Wyoming — Cities and the capital — Famous citizens — Wyoming's landscape — Grand Teton National Park — Yellowstone National Park — A history of Wyoming.
   ISBN 1-59197-709-6
      1. Wyoming—Juvenile literature. I. Title.

F761.3.M87 2005
978.7—dc22

                                                                 2005050117

Table Of Contents

A Snapshot Of Wyoming

Wyoming's landscape includes grasslands and prairies.

When people think of Wyoming, they think of wide-open spaces. This state has mountains, valleys, rivers, and forests. Even Wyoming's name refers to its landscape. It comes from a Native American word. The word means "upon the great plain."

There are 50 states in the United States. Every state is different. Every state has an official nickname. Wyoming's nickname is "The Equality State." This is because Wyoming allowed women to vote before any other state. Also, Wyoming's women served on juries and held public offices before those in other states.

Wyoming became the 44th state on July 10, 1890. Wyoming is the ninth-largest state in the United States. It has 97,818 square miles (253,347 sq km) of land. The state has a population of 493,782. That is the lowest population of all the states.

Where Is Wyoming?

There are four parts of the United States. Each part is called a region. Each region is in a different area of the country. The United States Census Bureau says the four regions are the Northeast, the South, the Midwest, and the West.

Wyoming is located in the West region of the United States. Wyoming has four seasons. The seasons are spring, summer, fall, and winter.

The temperatures are cooler in the higher parts of Wyoming's mountains.

Wyoming's weather is warm during the spring and summer months.

Four Regions of the United States of America

ALASKA

WASHINGTON

MONTANA

NORTH DAKOTA

VERMONT

MAINE

OREGON

IDAHO

MINNESOTA

WISCONSIN

NEW HAMPSHIRE

NEW YORK

MASSACHUSETTS

SOUTH DAKOTA

WYOMING

MICHIGAN

PENNSYLVANIA

RHODE ISLAND

CONNECTICUT

NEVADA

UTAH

COLORADO

NEBRASKA

IOWA

ILLINOIS

INDIANA

OHIO

NEW JERSEY

DELAWARE

Washington D.C.

CALIFORNIA

KANSAS

MISSOURI

WEST VIRGINIA

VIRGINIA

MARYLAND

KENTUCKY

NORTH CAROLINA

ARIZONA

NEW MEXICO

OKLAHOMA

ARKANSAS

TENNESSEE

SOUTH CAROLINA

MISSISSIPPI

ALABAMA

GEORGIA

TEXAS

LOUISIANA

FLORIDA

HAWAII

	West		Midwest		South		Northeast

Wyoming is bordered by six other states. Montana is north. South Dakota and Nebraska are east. Colorado is south. Utah borders Wyoming's southwest corner. And, Idaho is west.

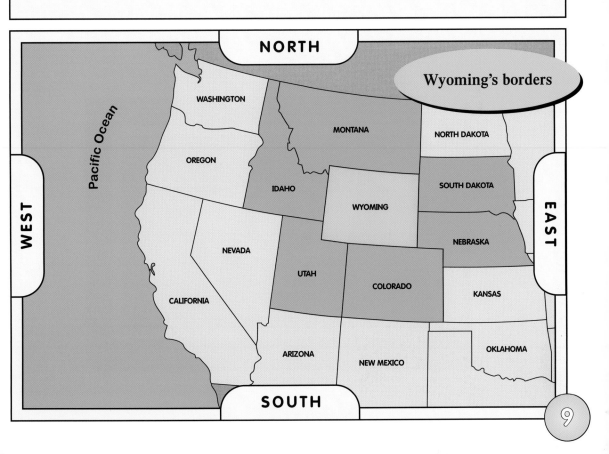

NORTH

Wyoming's borders

WASHINGTON

Pacific Ocean

MONTANA

NORTH DAKOTA

OREGON

IDAHO

WYOMING

SOUTH DAKOTA

WEST

EAST

NEVADA

UTAH

COLORADO

NEBRASKA

KANSAS

CALIFORNIA

ARIZONA

NEW MEXICO

OKLAHOMA

SOUTH

Wyoming

State abbreviation: WY

State nickname: The Equality State

State capital: Cheyenne

State motto: Equal Rights

Statehood: July 10, 1890, 44th state

Population: 493,782, ranks 50th

State flag:
Adopted in 1917

Land area: 97,818 square miles (253,347 sq km), ranks 9th

State tree: Cottonwood

State song: "Wyoming"

State government: Three branches: legislative, executive, and judicial

Average July temperature: 67°F (19°C)

Average January temperature: 19°F (-7°F)

State flower:
Indian paintbrush

State bird:
Meadowlark

State mammal:
Bison

Cities And The Capital

Cheyenne is the capital city of Wyoming. It is also the largest city in the state. Cheyenne is located in the southeast corner of Wyoming. Cheyenne is full of the history of the American West. This city is home to the Wyoming State Museum. There, people learn about the history of Wyoming through exhibits.

Casper is the second-largest city in Wyoming. Casper sits along the banks of the North Platte River. Many pioneers traveling west passed through Casper. The city was established in the 1850s as a military post on the Oregon Trail. Many people traveled west on the Oregon Trail.

Today, Casper has many oil refineries. They process oil into gas for cars and for heating.

Wyoming's State Capitol

Famous Citizens

Dick Cheney (1941–)

Dick Cheney was born in Nebraska in 1941. But, he grew up in Casper. Later, he represented Wyoming in the United States Congress. In 2000, Cheney was elected vice president of the United States. He ran with President George W. Bush. They were elected again in 2004.

Dick Cheney

Famous Citizens

Esther Hobart Morris (1814–1902)

Esther Hobart Morris was born in New York in 1814. She moved to Wyoming in 1868. Morris lived in South Pass City, Wyoming. She is famous for being the first female justice of the peace in the United States. This happened in 1870. She also fought for voting rights for women. There is a statue to honor her in the United States Capitol in Washington, D.C.

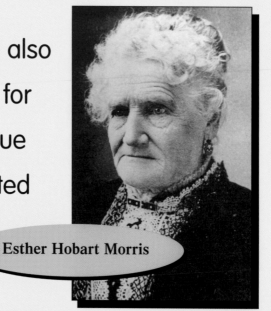

Esther Hobart Morris

Devils Tower

Devils Tower is a vertical rock formation. It is 1,267 feet (386 m) tall. Devils Tower is located in Wyoming, near the Belle Fourche River.

Devils Tower was the first national monument in the United States. President Theodore Roosevelt made this official on September 24, 1906.

A view of Devils Tower.

Today, people can walk around the base of Devils Tower. There, they can learn about its history.

The rock formation of Devils Tower is special to the Native American people.

Grand Teton National Park

Grand Teton National Park is located in northwestern Wyoming. It attracts many visitors each year. The Teton mountain range is part of the Rocky Mountains.

Grand Teton National Park has high snow-capped mountain peaks. Grand Teton peak is the highest point in the park at 13,770 feet (4,197 m). Jackson Hole is located at the base of the Teton Mountains.

A view of the Teton Mountains.

Grand Teton National Park has many miles of trails to explore. There are lakes and rivers for fishing and white-water rafting. Camping, biking, horseback riding, and snow skiing are also popular activities.

Wildlife in Grand Teton National Park includes moose, elks, bison, and bears.

Jenny Lake is a famous lake in Grand Teton National Park.

Yellowstone National Park

Wyoming is home to Yellowstone National Park. This was the first national park in the United States. Yellowstone became a national park in 1872. Today, Yellowstone is a popular place for people to visit.

A waterfall in Yellowstone National Park.

Mountains are one feature in Yellowstone's landscape.

Yellowstone National Park is located in the northwest corner of Wyoming. The park covers more than 2,200,000 acres (890,000 ha) of land. This park is known for its many different features.

One unique feature is Yellowstone's geysers. There are hundreds of geysers in the park. A geyser is formed when water seeps through cracks in the earth. Volcanic rock deep in the earth heats up the water, and it begins to boil. Then, the boiling water is pushed out of the earth in what looks like a spray.

"Old Faithful" is a famous geyser at Yellowstone National Park. Some people say that Old Faithful has sprayed at regular times for more than 80 years.

Yellowstone National Park is home to many different animals. Antelope, moose, wolves, deer, elks, bighorn sheep, and bears all live in the park.

A view of Old Faithful.

Wyoming

1803: President Thomas Jefferson arranges for the United States to buy Wyoming as part of the Louisiana Purchase.

1807: Trapper John Colter arrives in Wyoming.

1834: Fort William is built. This fort will later be called Fort Laramie.

1867: Union Pacific Railroad arrives in Wyoming.

1869: Wyoming passes a law that gives women rights to vote, to hold public offices, and to be part of juries.

1870: Esther Hobart Morris becomes the first female justice of the peace in the United States.

1872: Yellowstone National Park is established as the United States's first national park.

1890: Wyoming becomes the 44th state on July 10.

1906: Devils Tower becomes Devils Tower National Monument. It is the first national monument in the United States.

1925: Nellie Tayloe Ross of Wyoming becomes the first female governor in the United States.

1988: Fires sweep through parts of Yellowstone National Park. They are allowed to burn off naturally.

2000: Dick Cheney of Wyoming is elected vice president of the United States. George W. Bush is elected president.

2004: Cheney and Bush are elected for a second term.

George W. Bush (left) and Dick Cheney (right).

Cities In Wyoming

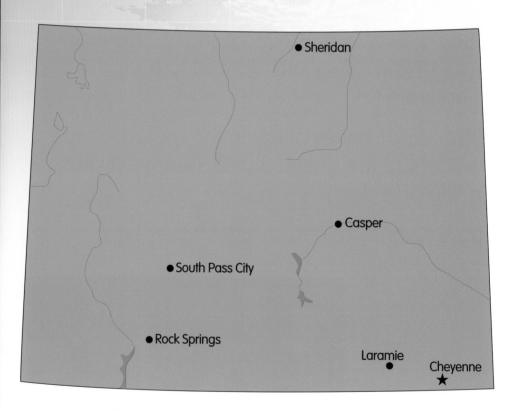

Important Words

capital a city where government leaders meet.

geyser a spring that boiling water pushes out of the earth.

Louisiana Purchase a deal where the United States bought land from France. Part of this land later became Wyoming.

nickname a name that describes something special about a person or a place.

pioneers people who traveled across the United States in the 1800s to settle the western United States.

Web Sites

To learn more about Wyoming, visit ABDO Publishing Company on the World Wide Web. Web site links about Wyoming are featured on our Book Links page. These links are routinely monitored and updated to provide the most current information available.

www.abdopub.com

Index